D0210834

The North American Indians

The
Sioux

Charles George

KIDHAVEN
PRESS™

THOMSON

GALE

San Diego • Detroit • New York • San Francisco • Cleveland
New Haven, Conn. • Waterville, Maine • London • Munich

LIBRARY OF CONGRESS CATALOGING-IN-PUBLICATION DATA

George, Charles, 1949–
  The Sioux / by Charles George.
    p. cm. — (North American Indians)
Summary: Discusses the Sioux people, their customs, family, organizations, food, gathering, religion, war, housing, and other aspects of daily life.
Includes bibliographical references and index.
  ISBN 0-7377-1513-8 (hardback: alk. paper)
  1. Dakota Indians—Juvenile literature. [1. Dakota Indians. 2. Indians of North America—Great Plains.] I. Title. II. Series.
  E99.D1G36 2004
  978.004'9752—dc21

                                                  2002155182

Contents

Chapter One

The People

Most people picture Indians of the American West as noble warriors—strong and brave, living in **tepees** and riding horses across the open plain in search of buffalo. Perhaps better than any other tribe, this image describes the people history knows as the Sioux. Those people did not call themselves the Sioux, however, and they did not always live on the Great Plains. They also had no written language. So, most of what we know about them comes from others. They did, however, have a rich tradition of storytelling, and they passed stories of their history from generation to generation.

What's in a Name?

Originally they called themselves Ocheti shakowin, or "Seven Council Fires," because there were seven main divisions of the tribe: Mdewkanton, Wahpeton, Wahpekute, Sisseton, Yankton, Yanktonai, and Teton. In later years, and today, the people known to history as the Sioux referred to themselves as Nakota, Lakota, or Dakota, depending on which branch they belong to. These words all mean "allies" or "friends."

Like many Indians, though, the Sioux received the name by which Americans know them because of a

A Sioux tribe member performs a ritual. Much of what we know of the Sioux comes from the tribe's own stories.

misunderstanding. When French explorers and trappers first came to the area west of the Great Lakes, they traded with the tribes living there. One of these tribes, the Chippewa, had always considered the Seven Council Fires their enemies. So, when Frenchmen asked Chippewa leaders for the name of the Seven Council Fires tribe, the Chippewa called them Nadowe-is-iw, meaning "snakes" or "enemies." The French thought this was the tribe's name and spelled it *Nadouessioux*. Later it was shortened to *Sioux*.

The earliest written mention of the Sioux appeared during the late 1600s and early 1700s. These accounts describe them as woodland Indians because they lived in forests along the Mississippi River, in what is now southern Minnesota, northwestern Wisconsin, and northeastern Iowa. According to those early accounts, the

A Sioux village alongside a river. The Sioux lived in tepees, portable shelters made from buffalo hide.

The Sioux were forced from the Great Lakes area by their enemies, the Chippewa, and they moved west to the Great Plains.

Sioux lived in bark-covered huts called wigwams. And they ate mostly berries, wild rice, fish, and small game they hunted on foot.

Moving to the Plains

During the mid-1700s Sioux history changed when their enemies, the Chippewa, received guns from the French. Without guns of their own to defend themselves against Chippewa attacks, the Sioux were forced to leave the Great Lakes area. Some groups moved south or northwest. But most Sioux moved west, across the Missouri River and onto the Great Plains.

The vast, open land must have seemed strange to the first Sioux who arrived there. The Great Plains was made up of miles of grass and had few trees. The Sioux called the Great Plains *oblayela,* "wideness of the world." Its emptiness gave those who lived there a sense of freedom not shared by forest dwellers.

In addition, the plains provided much of what the Sioux needed to survive. Millions of buffalo roamed freely across the prairie. Sometimes the huge herds stretched from horizon to horizon. The prairie was also home to millions of birds, whose songs filled the open air.

Food for the Soul, Too

The Great Plains gave the Sioux more than food. The land also provided many things the Indians could use to express their religious beliefs. Besides wild game, the prairies provided sage and other herbs used by Sioux spiritual healers called medicine men. Rivers crossed the plains, too—the Missouri, Platte, Cheyenne, and White. In many places, these rivers were lined with cottonwood trees that were sacred to the Sioux.

In addition to the vast, open areas of grasslands, the Great Plains contained places the Sioux considered mystical. One area, called the Badlands, had many odd earth formations and landscapes littered with fossils. The Sioux called the Badlands *mako sika,* "strange lands of the world," and avoided it. They believed ghosts and monsters lived there.

West of the Badlands, near present-day Rapid City, South Dakota, lies an area considered holy by the Sioux. They called it Paha Sapa, or "Black Hills." To the Sioux, these mountains were sacred. The Sioux believed Harney Peak, the area's tallest mountain, was the center of the universe.

Arrival of the Horse

With such a vast area to inhabit, the Sioux would have been lost if they had not acquired horses. Horses had been introduced to North America by Spanish explorers during the 1500s and 1600s. By the mid-1700s, horses traded or stolen from the Spanish were brought to the Great Plains. Plains Indians, having never seen horses, did not have words in their languages for these animals. So the Sioux called them *Shunka Wakan,* "Sacred Dog," "Medicine Dog," or "God Dog."

Horses transformed the Sioux way of life. The animals made the Sioux more mobile. Before getting horses, the Indians struggled to move from place to place. They had to carry their possessions on their backs or on sleds pulled by dogs. This made traveling very slow. Horses, however, could easily carry the heavy loads. This allowed the Sioux to move much faster.

The Sioux avoided the Badlands, an area in the Great Plains with many fossils (inset). They believed ghosts occupied the land.

Horses also changed the way the Sioux hunted. Hunters now chased herds of buffalo on horseback rather than on foot. Thus, instead of going hungry some of the time, the Sioux could catch enough food in a few days to feed their tribes for months. More successful hunts also meant more buffalo hides. The Sioux used these for clothing, shelter, and to preserve their history.

Tales Around the Campfire

Around campfires in Sioux winter camps, wise men of the tribe told stories to the young. The men often drew pictures on hides to illustrate their stories. Some of the stories were about mythical figures and how they brought things

The Sioux used hides with pictures like this one to help tell stories around the campfire.

to the tribe, such as fire or ways to track wild game. Others told how the tribe began. The next night, the men asked children to repeat these stories. Children enjoyed this challenging memory game. And, by participating in it, they learned about their tribe's traditions, religious beliefs, and history.

The Sioux also used buffalo hides to record the tribe's history. These records are called **winter counts**. On one special hide, the Sioux painted a small picture each year to document a major event. Hooflike symbols were for 1796, "Winter of Horse-Stealing Camp," when tribes raided each other for horses. A face covered with red dots meant "Winter When the People Died of Smallpox" in the year 1810. A shooting star recorded a meteor seen in 1821 and a meteor shower in 1834. With the arrival of the white man on the Great Plains during the early 1800s, images of men in black hats appeared on the hides.

These winter counts were carefully guarded for generations. They became permanent records of the tribe's life and sometimes spanned more than one hundred years. Although many of these hides were lost or destroyed over the years, some survived. These provide historians a glimpse of early Sioux life.

Winter counts, a rich tradition of storytelling, and the writings of people who came in contact with them, provide a complete and vivid story of the life of the Sioux. From humble beginnings in the forests of Minnesota, the Sioux had an important impact on the history of the American West.

Chapter Two

Daily Life on the Northern Plains

The Sioux who moved to the Great Plains adopted a lifestyle similar to other Plains Indian tribes. Like most Plains Indians, the Sioux had no strong central government to enforce their ideas of right and wrong. Instead, their behavior was controlled by well-established social customs.

Tribal Organization

The Plains Sioux lived on most of the land that is now North and South Dakota, eastern Montana, northeastern Wyoming, northern Nebraska, and western Minnesota. Despite this large area, the Sioux had no central government. No single leader spoke for the Sioux Nation. Instead, each band, or group, had its own chief.

This chief was by no means an all-powerful leader. He did not rule his band. He influenced the lives of his people, but they did not have to follow his advice. Rather, he served as an adviser and arbitrator. He suggested actions the band should take. He might make suggestions about where to hunt and where to camp. He also helped resolve arguments between band members.

During the summer, several bands met to choose a tribal council from leaders of the various bands. These councils decided when and against whom to make war, where to hunt for buffalo, and other issues that affected the tribe. Again, though, tribal members could accept the council's advice or reject it.

Sioux Camps

One of the most important decisions members of the tribal council made was when and where to move the tribe's camp. Because their main source of food, the buffalo, traveled across the prairie, the Sioux adopted a nomadic way of life. This meant the tribe was constantly on the move. Everything tribespeople owned had to be easy to move, even their homes.

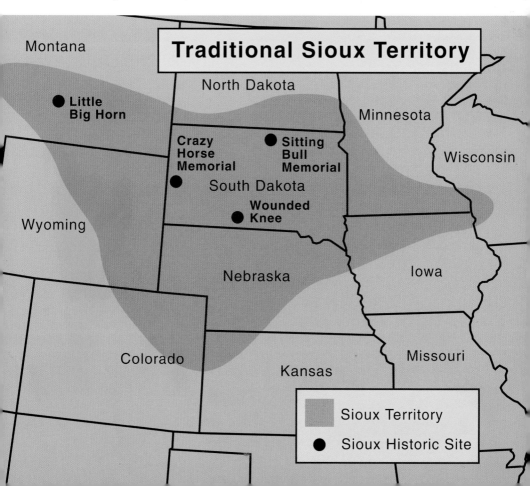

Traditional Sioux Territory

Montana

North Dakota

Minnesota

● Little Big Horn

Wisconsin

Crazy Horse Memorial

● Sitting Bull Memorial

●

South Dakota

Wounded ● Knee

Wyoming

Nebraska

Iowa

Colorado

Kansas

Missouri

Sioux Territory

● Sioux Historic Site

The Sioux's home on the Great Plains was a cone-shaped structure called a tepee. To build a tepee, Sioux women laid twelve to fifteen poles in a circle on the ground. They tied the poles together at one end, stood the framework up, spread the bases of the poles into a circle about fourteen feet in diameter, and secured the lower ends of the poles into the ground. On this framework, the Sioux women spread buffalo hides. They left a hole at the top for smoke to escape and an opening in the side as an entrance.

The tepee provided a comfortable place to live in every season. During winter, the Sioux hung a second layer of hides inside the tepee. This kept the home warm. In hotter months, the Sioux rolled up the sides of the tepee to allow fresh air inside for cooling.

Typically, Sioux bands camped beside rivers or streams, so they would have enough fresh water. Because

Sioux men drive buffalo from a cliff. The tribe used buffalo for food, clothing, and household items.

The tepee provided shelter for the Sioux during all kinds of weather.

they considered the circle a sacred image, the Sioux usually arranged their tepees in circles near those water sources. In addition, most Sioux tepees faced east to greet the morning sun.

Chores

In Sioux camps, men and women each had duties. Men were responsible for hunting and protecting the village.

15

They participated in council meetings and made the tribe's weapons—bows, arrows, and shields. Women did most of the other work. They cooked, made clothing, cared for the children, and set up camp.

It was the women's responsibility to make most of the items the family needed. Many of these things came from the buffalo. Sioux women dried a buffalo bladder to use as a water bag. The buffalo's stomach became a cooking pot. Horns were scraped out and used as bowls, cups, and spoons. Bones became scrapers and other tools. Slivers of bone were made into needles for sewing, and the animal's sinews served as thread.

The buffalo's skin and hair were especially useful. Women used buffalo hides to make warm robes, clothing, shoes, and blankets. They sewed as many as fifteen hides together to cover a tepee. They cut hides into strips and braided them into ropes. Buffalo hair could also be braided into rope or used to stuff pillows. And fly swatters could be made from the tails.

Fancy Needlework

During winter months most groups settled in one place, and women had time for artistic projects such as beadwork and quillwork. They sewed wooden beads, porcupine quills, bird quills, grasses, bits of fur, and small animal bones into patterns on their best clothing. Decorated clothes were reserved for special occasions. These included religious ceremonies, tribal councils, and **powwows**, annual gatherings of the tribe.

Sioux women worked hard, but they were not slaves to their husbands. In fact, they had a good deal of influence in the tribe's affairs. They were free to express their opinions to their husbands and at tribal councils. They also took part in religious ceremonies and rituals alongside the men.

During the cold winter months Sioux women spent much of their time doing beadwork (inset).

Tools for Worship and for War

Sioux men also spent the colder months crafting items important to the tribe. They made drums, smoking pipes, warbonnets, shields, spears, bows, and arrows. Craftsmen with special skills created some of these items. But almost every man made his own arrows, bow, and shield.

Sioux men made arrows from various kinds of wood, but they preferred gooseberry, cherry, or Juneberry. They shaped and straightened arrows by pulling and twisting them through holes in sandstone. Then they glued on wild turkey or buzzard feathers to make the arrows fly straight.

To make a bow, a Sioux warrior chose a strong, flexible piece of wood. He wrapped the wood tightly with leather thongs. This helped prevent the wood from splintering and made the bow stronger. Then he made a bowstring from shredded buffalo sinew and stretched it onto the bow.

In addition to his bow and arrows, a Sioux warrior's war shield was very important in battle. To make a shield, a warrior stretched three or four layers of wet, tough buffalo hide across a wooden frame. Next, he stuffed furs between the layers. Finally, the hides were allowed to dry. As they did, the hides shrank onto the framework and hardened. A well-made shield could deflect a spear, an arrow, or even a bullet.

A butcher cuts deer meat with a sharpened rock. Sioux hunters used sharpened rock to make many weapons and tools.

A Sioux woman uses a wooden tool to stretch a fresh animal hide.

Family Values

When not hunting or making things the tribe needed, most Sioux enjoyed spending time with friends and family. To the Sioux, family was very important. Fathers and sons showed each other a great deal of respect, as did mothers and daughters.

That respect and honor was nowhere more apparent than in how Sioux families raised their children. Sioux parents taught their children to respect their elders; to be generous, honest, and brave; and to value hard work.

These traits were very important because life on the Great Plains was hard. There was much work to be done, and life in a Sioux village demanded respect and cooperation.

19

Chapter Three

The Spirit World

R eligion dominated almost every Sioux thought and activity. The spirit world controlled how they lived and explained where they came from.

Like most cultures, the Sioux had a rich **mythology**. One legend had to do with how the Black Hills were formed during a footrace between man and the animals. Another explained the origin of huge fossilized dinosaur bones they discovered. At the heart of each legend, though, was the belief in a power greater than man.

Wakan Tanka, One and Many

To the Sioux, everything, including man, was part of nature. And nature was the product of a kind, creative force called Wakan Tanka, the "Great Mystery" or the "Big Holy." According to Luther Standing Bear, a Sioux born in 1868,

> The Indian loved to worship. From birth to death, he revered [respected] his surroundings. He considered himself born in the luxurious lap of Mother Earth, and no place was, to him, humble [ordinary, or lowly]. The blessings of *Wakan Tanka* flowed over the Indian like rain showered from the sky. *Wakan*

A Sioux medicine man stands in prayer at the top of a cliff. The Sioux held deep beliefs in the power of the spirit world.

Tanka was not aloof, apart. He did not punish the animals and the birds, and likewise, he did not punish man. He was not a punishing god. There was but one ruling power, and that was Good. [1]

Wakan Tanka was actually more than a single god. He represented many gods, combined into one. This was because the Sioux recognized gods all around them.

Sioux men perform a religious ceremony. The tribe believed in many gods, all combined into one creative force.

Most of these gods were good. They watched over the tribe and provided strength and inspiration. Of these, Wi, the sun, held the highest rank. He appeared every day and represented bravery, strength, generosity, and loyalty. Other Sioux gods were Skan, the sky; Maka, the earth; Inyan, the rock; Tate, the wind; and Tatanka, the buffalo god.

Sioux medicine men often created religious objects, called **fetishes**, to symbolize these gods on Earth. The Sioux believed these fetishes would protect them from harm. A fetish for Maka might be anything that grew from the soil—a bundle of sage or grass, perhaps. Anything hard as stone might serve as a fetish for Inyan. And a buffalo skull could represent Tatanka.

The Sioux also recognized evil gods, who brought trouble to people. The Mini Watu, for example, caused things to rot, and were always trying to enter the human body. If they were successful, a person might become ill. If that person died from the illness, the Sioux believed the Mini Watu had driven Niya, a person's spirit, from the body. The Sioux believed that every misfortune was the result of one of their evil gods.

The Vision Quest

The Sioux sought the power to combat the evil gods from Wakan Tanka. They began seeking this power at an early age in a ceremony they called *hanbleceyapi,* the **vision quest**.

About the age of twelve, most Sioux boys—and some girls—went out alone to discover their spirit guides. These guides were something in nature that would teach them lessons about life. To find the guides, the young Sioux walked far away from camp, usually to an isolated hilltop. There, they went without food for four days, prayed, sometimes tortured themselves, and asked the gods to send a sign, called a vision, that would give them power.

During this time, the seeker watched for anything out of the ordinary that might be a sign from the gods. It could be a uniquely shaped stone, a thunderstorm, a shooting star, or a particular animal. If a wolf came nearby, for example, the young Sioux might interpret it as his spirit guide. He then might carry some part of a wolf—an ear or tail, for example—as a symbol of his spiritual connection to that animal. This item would become his most prized possession. He would carry it with him always.

The Sweat Lodge

Another ceremony that helped Sioux men and women find the wisdom and guidance of Wakan Tanka was the sweat lodge ceremony, or *Inipi*. In this ceremony, people entered a tent made specifically for this purpose and sat in a circle. Heated stones were brought into the tent, and water was sprinkled on them to make steam. This process was supposed to purify the spirits and bodies of those participating so they could better communicate with the gods.

The leader of the ceremony entered the lodge first. He brought a sacred pipe for everyone to smoke. He also prayed and made an offering to the gods. Then, others (usually four people) entered the lodge and sat in a circle. They also smoked the pipe and prayed.

After each person had smoked, a flap was lowered across the tent's opening. This plunged everyone inside into darkness and symbolized their ignorance. When the flap was finally opened and the participants emerged, they believed they had been reborn and had left ignorance behind. The sweat ritual was very important to the Sioux. They always practiced it before any major event,

Sioux tribe members participate in the Sun Dance, an annual religious ceremony.

Cross Section of a Tepee

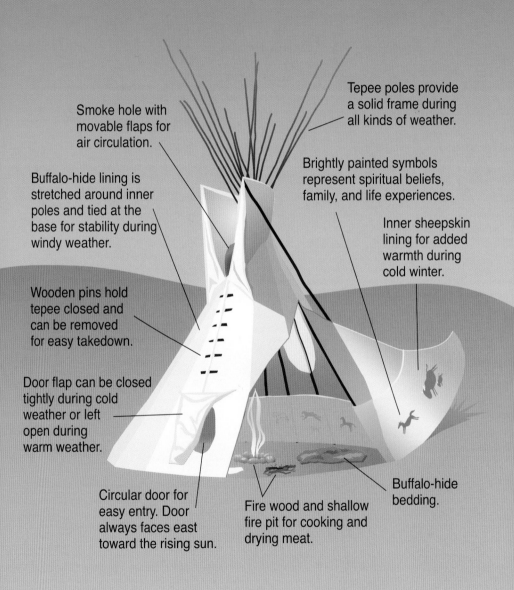

Smoke hole with movable flaps for air circulation.

Tepee poles provide a solid frame during all kinds of weather.

Buffalo-hide lining is stretched around inner poles and tied at the base for stability during windy weather.

Brightly painted symbols represent spiritual beliefs, family, and life experiences.

Inner sheepskin lining for added warmth during cold winter.

Wooden pins hold tepee closed and can be removed for easy takedown.

Door flap can be closed tightly during cold weather or left open during warm weather.

Buffalo-hide bedding.

Circular door for easy entry. Door always faces east toward the rising sun.

Fire wood and shallow fire pit for cooking and drying meat.

such as a war party, a buffalo hunt, or the making of a treaty.

Sacred Objects

In the sweat lodge, and in other ceremonies, the Sioux used two objects—the drum and the pipe. Sioux holy man Black Elk once said that the drum's shape, a circle, "represents the universe, and its steady strong beat is the pulse, the heart. . . . As the voice of *Wakan Tanka,* it . . . helps us to understand the mystery and the power of things." [2]

The pipe, on the other hand, carried prayers to Wakan Tanka. According to legend, the pipe came to the Sioux from a beautiful maiden called White Buffalo Calf Woman. She appeared long ago, bringing a pipe made of reddish stone and wood. This pipe had a buffalo carved on the side and twelve eagle feathers hanging from it. The maiden told the Sioux it symbolized the earth, everything that grows on the earth, and the animals and birds that live here. She also told them that no one who smoked the pipe could tell a lie.

The Sun Dance

The Sioux used drums and ceremonial pipes in their most dramatic religious ceremony—the Sun Dance. During this annual four-day event, usually held in late spring or early summer, the participants did not eat any food. Then, they danced around a pole and looked in the general direction of the sun for hours or even days. When exhausted dancers collapsed, their relatives dragged them into the shade. A person who went through this ordeal did so to symbolically take on the pain of others in his tribe. That way, they would not have to suffer.

Some Sioux warriors also used this ceremony to make extreme physical sacrifices to the gods. These warriors pierced the flesh of their chests with a knife and put wooden rods through the cuts. Leather thongs were then tied from these rods to the central pole. The warriors danced around the pole and pulled away until the rods

A Sioux warrior pierces his flesh during the Sun Dance. This was done as a sacrifice to the gods.

A Sioux grave is decorated with bison skulls representing the buffalo god Tatanka.

ripped through their skin. The warriors believed that, by suffering in this way, they took on the suffering of their people.

Belief in the spirit world was central to Sioux culture. The Sioux believed that if they did what the gods told them to and took part in ceremonies such as vision quests, dances, and the sweat lodge, they would live long and happy lives.

Chapter Four

The Coming of the White Man

The Sioux's religion prepared them for life on the Great Plains. But nothing prepared them for the arrival on the plains of a new people—the *Wasichu*—the white man. White traders and trappers had indirectly caused the Sioux's migration onto the Great Plains during the 1700s, when they sold guns to the Chippewa. Despite this, the Sioux lived in relative peace for more than one hundred years.

Then, in the early 1800s, whites again put pressure on the Sioux by moving onto their lands. The U.S. government wanted to expand the country's borders westward. But Sioux lands lay in its path.

Early Conflicts, Treaties, and Broken Promises

From 1851 to 1868, white settlers crossing Sioux lands faced attacks from the tribe. Because of this, the U.S. Army built forts along the trails to protect settlers. Sioux leaders and U.S. representatives also signed several treaties in an effort to stop the violence. But each time, promises were broken, and conflicts began again.

Finally, in 1868 the United States held talks with Red Cloud, a Sioux chief, at Fort Laramie, in what is now southeastern Wyoming. During the talks, Red Cloud insisted the government abandon the forts and leave the area. In return, he agreed to take his people to a **reservation** established for them in the Black Hills. This area, called the Great Sioux Reservation, included the western half of what is now South Dakota. The U.S. government agreed and promised that the Sioux could also hunt buffalo near the Powder River. This river is just west of the Black Hills in what is today northern Wyoming and southern Montana. U.S. officials signed the treaty, and they promised that the Black Hills would be Sioux land "for as long as the grass shall grow." [3]

U.S. soldiers raid an Indian village. The arrival of white settlers disrupted the peaceful life of the Sioux.

Custer and the Little Bighorn

After only six years, though, the U.S. government broke this promise. In 1874 rumors of gold in the Black Hills brought thousands of whites to Sioux land. When the Sioux complained, the United States offered to buy the land. Sioux leaders refused to sell.

In late 1875 the U.S. government issued an order that all Sioux had to leave much of the Powder River area. The tribe refused, and both sides prepared for war. Leading the Sioux was Sitting Bull, a medicine man. His war chief was a warrior named Crazy Horse.

Sitting Bull, a Sioux medicine man, led his tribe in protecting their lands from the U.S. government.

The Sioux defeat George Custer and his army at the Battle of the Little Bighorn in 1876.

In the spring of 1876, the U.S. Army marched into the Powder River area. On June 25, 1876, Lieutenant Colonel George Armstrong Custer and his 225 men attacked a group of Sioux braves near the Little Bighorn River, in what is now southeastern Montana. They did this before the rest of the U.S. force was ready. This decision cost them their lives. In less than an hour, Crazy Horse and his braves defeated Custer's forces. Whites called this battle Custer's Last Stand, or the Battle of the Little Bighorn. The Sioux called it the Battle of Greasy Grass.

Giving Up the Old Way of Life

Despite this victory, the Sioux soon met defeat. News of the battle at the Little Bighorn outraged the U.S. government. In response, over the next months U.S. forces chased and captured band after band of Sioux. The government then herded the Sioux onto one of seven reservations in South Dakota.

The Sioux would have continued to resist, but they were starving. During this period, whites had begun hunting buffalo on the plains. Some hunters killed more than one hundred animals a day. Soon, the prairie was littered with skeletons and rotting carcasses.

In 1850 an estimated 50 million buffalo had roamed the plains. By 1885, there were none. The Sioux's primary source of food was gone. Starvation finally forced the remaining Sioux bands onto the reservations.

Reservation life was very strange to the Sioux. They had always roamed free and hunted for food. On the reservation, though, they were treated as prisoners and guarded by U.S. soldiers. Some reservations were even surrounded by barbed-wire fences. And the Sioux's weapons and most of their horses were taken away.

On the reservation, Sioux warriors were made to live in log cabins and told to become farmers. They had to depend on their own crops for food. But because they had never been farmers before, the crops often failed. When that happened, they had to take government handouts to survive.

Ghost Dances and Wounded Knee

The Sioux had not yet accepted defeat, though. Looking again to their religious beliefs, the Sioux made one last attempt to regain their way of life. In the winter of 1890 a medicine man named Kicking Bear introduced the

The Sioux perform the Ghost Dance, a special ceremony the tribe believed would make the white settlers leave.

Ghost Dance to the Sioux reservations. Kicking Bear had learned of this special ceremony from Wovoka, a young Paiute Indian in Nevada. Wovoka had dreamed that the plains tribes could return to their old way of life if they stopped fighting the whites and performed the Ghost Dance.

Dancer Steve Yellowhawk performs during a traditional Sioux powwow.

As a result of this story, hundreds of Sioux danced and chanted on the reservations. Government officials, though, worried that all the activity was the beginning of an uprising. So they sent troops to stop the dancing. More than three hundred of the Ghost Dancers fled toward the Pine Ridge Reservation in southwestern South Dakota. They thought they would be safe there.

U.S. troops followed and caught up to the group on December 28, 1890, and the Sioux surrendered. Then the troops ordered the Indians to spend the night camping in the freezing cold along Wounded Knee Creek.

Early the following morning, five hundred U.S. soldiers surrounded the camp and opened fire. They killed at least 150 Sioux, including women and children who were running away from the fight. This event, called the Massacre at Wounded Knee, brought an end to Ghost Dancing. It also ended any dreams the Sioux had of returning to their old way of life.

The Sioux Today

Today, the state of South Dakota is home to nine Sioux reservations. These are Pine Ridge, Rosebud, Cheyenne River, Crow Creek, Flandreau Santee, Lower Brulé, Sisseton-Wahpeton, Standing Rock, and Yankton. Most of the approximately sixty thousand Sioux who live in South Dakota make their homes on these reservations. Every year, each reservation holds a powwow to teach younger generations about Sioux history, language, and culture. Reservations also fund tribal colleges.

The Sioux are also carving a huge monument to Crazy Horse in southwestern South Dakota. The monument, begun during the 1940s, has been financed entirely by private donations and is still under construction. In 1998, sculptors completed Crazy Horse's face. It is as tall as a nine-story building. When the carving is finished, it

When completed, the huge Crazy Horse monument will be the largest
sculpture in the world.

will be 641 feet long and will stand 560 feet tall. This
will make it the largest sculpture in the world.

Life on today's reservations is not easy. The Sioux still
face hardships. Alcoholism, drug use, illiteracy, and suicide
rates are much higher on reservations than among
America's general population. And most people living on
reservations are poor. Despite this, the Sioux remain strong.
And they continue to work for a positive future.

Notes

Chapter Three: The Spirit World

1. Quoted in Editors of Time-Life Books, *The Spirit World.* Alexandria, VA: Time-Life Books, 1992, p. 11.
2. Quoted in Editors of Time-Life Books, *The Spirit World,* p. 149.

Chapter Four: The Coming of the White Man

3. Quoted in Jon E. Lewis, *The Mammoth Book of the West.* New York: Carroll & Graf, 1996, p. 415.

Glossary

fetish: An object believed by ancient people to have magical powers to protect or provide help for its owner.

mythology: A collection of stories that expresses the beliefs of a group of people, telling about gods or goddesses, or giving reasons for something that happens in nature, such as thunder.

powwow: An American Indian social gathering, usually with ceremonial dancing, singing, games, and feasts.

reservation: An area of land set aside by the government for a special purpose, such as a place for American Indians to live together.

tepee: A cone-shaped, portable shelter made from poles and buffalo hides or canvas.

vision quest: A ceremony practiced by American Indian boys, and sometimes girls, upon reaching a certain age, to obtain spiritual power from something in nature—animals, weather, etc.

winter counts: A special buffalo hide kept by Sioux elders on which they painted pictures to show the tribe's history.

For Further Exploration

Books

Sally Senzell Isaacs, *Life in a Sioux Village.* Portsmouth, NH: Heinemann Library, 2001. The author provides a look at daily life in a Sioux village—clothing, food, activities, and homes.

E. Barrie Kavasch, *Lakota Sioux Children and Elders Talk Together.* New York: Rosen, 1999. This book explores the land, culture, traditions, and current status of the Sioux on the Pine Ridge Reservation in South Dakota through the voices of a young girl and several elders.

Rachel A. Koestler-Grack, *Sioux: Nomadic Buffalo Hunters.* Mankato, MN: Capstone, 2003. This work discusses the Sioux Indians, focusing on their tradition of hunting bison. It includes a recipe for pemmican, an Indian food made from berries and animal fat, and instructions for making a paper buffalo robe.

Bill Lund, *The Sioux Indians.* Mankato, MN: Capstone, 1997. This book provides an overview of the past and present lives of the Sioux, covering their daily life, customs, relations with the government and others, and more.

Ann McGovern, *If You Lived with the Sioux Indians.* New York: Scholastic, 1999. McGovern describes the daily life of the Sioux Indians—their clothing, food, games, and customs—before and after the coming of the white man.

Andrew Santella, *The Lakota Sioux.* New York: Scholastic, 2001. This work discusses the daily life, customs, traditions, and present status of the largest branch of the Sioux Nation.

Virginia Schomp, *Heroic Sioux Warrior: Crazy Horse.* Tarrytown, NY: Marshall Cavendish, 1998. A biography of the Oglala leader who steadfastly resisted the white man's attempt to take over Indian lands.

Diane Shaughnessy, *Sitting Bull: Courageous Sioux Chief.* New York: Rosen, 1997. A biography of the Sioux chief who, although he led his people into the Battle of the Little Bighorn, was also a man of mercy, wisdom, and peace.

Virginia Driving Hawk Sneve, *The Sioux.* New York: Holiday House, 1995. This book identifies the different tribes of the Sioux Indians and discusses their beliefs and traditional way of life.

Ann M. Todd, *Sioux: People of the Great Plains.* Mankato, MN: Capstone, 2002. An overview of the Sioux, focusing on their lives on the plains.

Caryn Yacowitz, *Sioux.* Portsmouth, NH: Heinemann Library, 2002. This work describes the history, social life, customs, and present status of the Sioux.

Websites

A Guide to the Great Sioux Nation (www.travelsd. com). A travel site sponsored by the state of South Dakota that contains links to the history of individual tribes and information about the state's Sioux reservations.

Plains Indian History (www.plainsindianhistory.com). A great site with lots of links to varied topics common to all Plains Indians. Contains information about the Battle of the Little Bighorn and the Massacre at Wounded Knee as well as short biographies of great chiefs.

Tracking the Buffalo (http://americanhistory.si.edu). The Smithsonian Institution sponsors this site devoted to the Plains Indians and the uses of the buffalo. Contains an interactive game for children, matching parts of a buffalo with tools made from those parts, and a section about painting buffalo hides with a reproducible page children can use to draw their own "winter count."

Index

Picture Credits

Cover: © CORBIS

© Blackbirch Press Photo Archive, 38

© CORBIS, 35

COREL Corporation, 9 (inset), 38 (inset)

Chris Jouan, 26

Library of Congress, 5, 21

© Nativestock.com, 10, 14, 17 (both), 18, 19, 25, 28, 32, 36

© North Wind Picture Archives, 6, 7, 15, 22, 29, 31, 33

PhotoDisc, 9

About the Author

Charles George taught history and Spanish in Texas public schools for sixteen years. He now lives with his wife of thirty-two years, Linda, in the mountains of New Mexico. Together, they have written more than forty young adult and children's nonfiction books. Charles has written two Lucent books, *Life Under the Jim Crow Laws* and *Civil Rights,* and three KidHaven books, including *The Holocaust,* part of the History of the World series, and *The Comanche,* for the North American Indians series. He and Linda also wrote *Texas* for the series Seeds of a Nation.